Elegaic sonnets, and other poems.

Charlotte Turner Smith

Dark gathering clouds involve &c.

SONNETS,

AND OTHER

POEMS,

BY

Charlotte Smith.

THE FIRST *WORCESTER* EDITION, FROM THE
SIXTH *LONDON* EDITION, WITH ADDITIONS.

PRINTED AT WORCESTER,

BY Isaiah Thomas,

SOLD BY HIM IN *WORCESTER*, AND BY SAID *THOMAS* AND
ANDREWS IN BOSTON.

1795.

TO **William Hayley,** ESQ.

SIR,

WHILE I ask your protection for these Essays, I cannot deny having myself some esteem for them. Yet permit me to say, that did I not trust to your candor and sensibility, and hope they will plead for the errors your judgment must discover, I should never have availed myself of the liberty I have obtained—that of dedicating these simple effusions to the greatest modern Master of that charming talent, in which I can never be more than a distant copyist.

I am, Sir,

Your most obedient and obliged servant,

CHARLOTTE SMITH.

PREFACE

TO THE

FIRST AND *SECOND* EDITIONS.

THE little Poems, which are here called Sonnets, have, I believe, no very just claim to that title : But they consist of fourteen lines, and appear to me no improper vehicle for a single Sentiment. I am told, and I read it as the opinion of very good judges, that the legitimate Sonnet is illy calculated for our language. The specimen Mr. Hayley has given, though they form a strong exception, prove no more, than that the difficulties of the attempt vanish before uncommon powers.

Some very melancholy moments have been beguiled, by expressing in verse the sensa-

A 2

tions

tions those moments brought. Some of my
friends, with partial indiscretion, have mul-
tiplied the copies they procured of several
of these attempts, till they found their way
into the prints of the day in a mutilated
state: which, concurring with other circumstances, determined me to put them into their
present form. I can hope for readers only
among the few, who to sensibility of heart,
join simplicity of taste.

PREFACE

TO THE

THIRD AND *FOURTH* EDITIONS.

THE reception given by the public, as well as my particular friends, to the two first Editions of these Poems, has induced me to add to the present such other Sonnets as I have written since, or have recovered from my acquaintance, to whom I had given them without thinking well enough of them at the time to preserve any copies myself. A few of those last written, I have attempted on the Italian model; with what success I know not, but I am persuaded that to the generality of readers those which are less regular will be more pleasing.

As

As a few notes were necefsary, I have added them at the end. I have there quoted such lines as I have borrowed ; and even where I am conscious the ideas were not my own, I have restored them to their original pofsefsors.

PREFACE

TO THE

SIXTH EDITION.

WHEN a sixth Edition of these little Poems was lately called for, it was proposed to me, to add such Sonnets or other pieces, as I might have written since the publication of the fifth.—Of these, however, I had only a few ; and on shewing them to a friend of whose judgment I had a high opinion, he remarked, that some of them, particularly 'The Sleeping Woodman,' and 'The Return of the Nightingale,' resembled in their subjects, and still more in the plaintive tone in which they are written, the greater part of those in the former Editions—and that, perhaps, some of a more lively cast, might be

better

better liked by the Public.—'Toujours perdrix,' said my friend, 'Toujours perdrix,'
you know, ' ne vaut rien.'—I am far from
supposing that *your* compositions can be neg-
lected or disapproved on whatever subject ;
but perhaps 'toujours Rofsignols, toujours
des chansons tristes,' may not be so well re-
ceived as if you attempted, what you would
certainly execute as succefsfully, a more
cheerful style of composition.—' Alas !' re-
plied I, ' Are grapes gathered from thorns,
or figs from thistles ?'—Or, Can the *effect*
cease, while the *cause* remains ? *You know* that
when in the Beech Woods of Hampshire, I
first struck the chords of the melancholy lyre,
its notes were never intended for the public
ear ! It was unaffected sorrows drew them
forth : I wrote mournfully because I was unhappy : And I have unfortunately no reason
yet,

yet, though nine years have since elapsed, to *change my tone.* The time is indeed arrived, when I have been promised by ' *the Honorable Men*' who *nine years ago,* undertook to see that my family obtained the provision their grandfather designed for them, that ' all should be well—all should be settled.' But still I am condemned to feel the ' *hope delayed that maketh the heart sick.*' Still to receive—not a repetition of promises indeed—*but of scorn and insult*; when I apply to those gentlemen, they will neither tell me *when* they will proceed to divide the estate ; or, *whether they will ever do so at all.* You know the circumstances under which I have now so long been laboring ; and you have done me the honor to say, that few women could so long have contended with them. With these, however, as they are some of them of a domestic and painful nature, I will

not

not trouble the public *now* ; but while they exist in all their force, that indulgent public must accept all I am able to atchieve—'Toujours des chansons tristes !'

Thus ended the short dialogue between my friend and me, and I repeat it as an apology for that apparent despondence, which when it is observed for a long series of years, may look like affectation. *I shall be sorry*, if on some future occasion, I should feel myself compelled to detail its causes more at length ; for notwithstanding I am thus frequently appearing as an authorefs, and have derived from thence many of the greatest advantages of my life, (since it has procured me friends whose attachment is most invaluable) I am well aware that for a woman—'The post of honor is a private station.'

London, May 14, 1792.

THE Editor of this (Worcester) Edition, intended to have published it nearly four years since, at which time he had the plates engraved in his Office in this town. His being employed in printing larger and heavier volumes has prevented these Sonnets appearing from his Press till now.—As the Letter Press has been delayed, he could have wished the Engravings had been also ; as in the infancy of engraving in this country, four years' additional experience to the artist would doubtless have produced more delicate work than what is now presented. The lovers of this Art will, however, be enabled, in some measure, to mark the progress of Engraving by a comparison of the Plates *now* executed with these, and the Editor doubts not but a proper allowance will be made for work engraved by an artist who obtained his knowledge in this country, by whom these plates were executed, and that done by European engravers who have settled in the United States.

The making of the particular kind of paper on which these Sonnets are printed, is a new business in America ; and but lately introduced into Greatbritain ; it is the first manufactured by the Editor.

On the whole, the Editor hopes for the candor of those who wish well to the productions of the Columbian Press—their favorable acceptance of this, and other volumes printed in this country, will doubtless raise an emulation to produce others, better executed, on superior paper, and with more delicate engravings.

ISAIAH THOMAS.

Worcester, Massachusetts, October, 1795.

B

CONTENTS.

.

SONNETS.

XLVIII.

Page.

OTHER POEMS.

Peasant

DIRECTIONS TO THE BINDER.

To place the Plates.

Dark gath'ring clouds, &c. to face Title Page. [*The reader
will note this plate belongs to the Elegy, page* 83]

Let the plates *face* the Sonnets to which they belong.—
Cut the book as large each way as it will bear.

ELEGIAC SONNETS.

SONNET I.

THE partial Muse has, from my earliest hours,
   Smil'd on the rugged path I'm doom'd to tread,
And still with sportive hand has snatch'd wild flow'rs,
   To weave fantastic garlands for my head:
But far, far happier is the lot of those
   Who never learn'd her dear delusive art;
Which, while it decks the head with many a rose,
   Reserves the thorn, to fester in the heart.
For still she bids soft Pity's melting eye
   Stream o'er the ills she knows not to remove,
Points ev'ry pang, and deepens ev'ry sigh
   Of mourning Friendship, or unhappy Love.
Ah! then, how dear the Muse's favors cost,
If those paint sorrow best—who feel it most. 14

SONNET II.

Written at the Close of Spring.

THE garlands fade that Spring so lately wove,
   Each simple flow'r, which she had nurs'd in dew,
Anemonies that spangled every grove, 3
   The primrose wan, and harebell, mildly blue.
No more shall violets linger in the dell,
   Or purple orchis variegate the plain,
Till Spring again shall call forth every bell,
   And drefs with humid hands her wreaths again.—
Ah, poor Humanity ! so frail, so fair,
   Are the fond visions of thy early day,
Till tyrant Pafsion, and corrosive Care,
   Bid all thy fairy colours fade away !
Another May new buds and flow'rs shall bring;
Ah ! Why has Happinefs—no second Spring ?

SONNET III.

To a Nightingale.

POOR melancholy bird—that all night long ɪ
  Tell'st to the Moon thy tale of tender woe;
  From what sad cause can such sweet sorrow flow,
And whence this mournful melody of song ᵃ

Thy poet's musing fancy would translate
  What mean the sounds that swell thy little breast,
  When still at dewy eve thou leav'st thy nest,
Thus to the list'ning night to sing thy fate ?

Pale Sorrow's victims wert thou once among,
  Tho' now releas'd in woodlands wild to rove ?
Say—Hast thou felt from friends some cruel wrong,
  Or diedst thou—martyr of disastrous love ᵃ
Ah, songstrefs sad ! that such my lot might be,
To sigh and sing, at liberty—like thee !

SONNET IV.

To the Moon.

QUEEN of the silver bow!—by thy pale beam,
   Alone and pensive, I delight to stray,
And watch thy shadow trembling in the stream,
   Or mark the floating clouds that crofs thy way.
And while I gaze, thy mild and placid light
   Sheds a soft calm upon my troubled breast;
And oft I think—fair planet of the night—
   That in thy orb, the wretched may have rest:
The suff'rers of the earth perhaps may go,
   Releas'd by Death—to thy benignant sphere,
And the sad children of Despair and Woe
   Forget, in thee, their cup of sorrow here.
Oh! that I soon may reach thy world serene,
Poor wearied pilgrim—in this toiling scene!

Queen of the Silver Bow &c ——

SONNET V.

To the South Downs.

AH, hills belov'd !—where once a happy child,

Your beechen shades, 'your turf, your flow'rs among,'
I wove your bluebells into garlands wild,

And woke your echoes with my artlefs song.
Ah, hills belov'd !—your turf, your flow'rs remain;

But, Can they peace to this sad breast restore ?
For one poor moment soothe the sense of pain,

And teach a breaking heart to throb no more ?
And you, Aruna !—in the vale below,

As to the sea your limpid waves you bear,
Can you one kind Lethean cup bestow,

To drink a long oblivion to my care ?
Ah, no !—when all, e'en Hope's last ray is gone,
There's no oblivion—but in Death alone !

C

SONNET VI.

To Hope.

OH, Hope ! thou soother sweet of human woes !
   How shall I lure thee to my haunts forlorn !
For me wilt thou renew the wither'd rose,
   And clear my painful path of pointed thorn ?
Ah come, sweet nymph ! in smiles and softnefs drest,
   Like the young hours that lead the tender year ;
Enchantrefs come ! and charm my cares to rest :—
   Alas ! the flatterer flies, and will not hear !
A prey to fear, anxiety and pain,
   Muft I a sad existence still deplore ?
Lo !—the flow'rs fade, but all the thorns remain,
   ' For me the vernal garland blooms no more.' 12
Come then ' pale Misery's love !' be thou my cure, 13
And I will blefs thee, who tho' slow art sure.

SONNET VII.

On the Departure of the Nightingale.

SWEET poet of the woods—a long adieu !
   Farewell, soft minstrel of the early year !
Ah ! 'twill be long ere thou shalt sing anew,
   And pour thy music on the ' night's dull ear.' 4
Whether on Spring thy wandering flights await, 5
   Or whether silent in our groves you dwell,
The pensive muse shall own thee for her mate, 7
   And still protect the song she loves so well.
With cautious step the lovelorn youth shall glide
   Thro' the lone brake that shades thy mofsy nest ;
And shepherd girls, from eyes profane shall hide
   The gentle bird, who sings of pity best ·
For still thy voice shall soft affections move,
And still be dear to sorrow, and to love !

SONNET VIII.

To Spring.

AGAIN the wood, and long withdrawing vale,
    In many a tint of tender green are drest,
Where the young leaves unfolding, scarce conceal,
    Beneath their early shade, the half form'd nest
Of finch or woodlark , and the primrose pale,
    And lavish cowslip, wildly scatter'd round,
Give their sweet spirits to the sighing gale.
    Ah, season of delight !—could aught be found
        To soothe awhile the tortur'd bosom's pain,
    Of Sorrow's rankling shaft to cure the wound,
        And bring life's first delusions once again,
'Twere surely met in thee !—thy prospect fair,
Thy sounds of harmony, thy balmy air,
Have power to cure all sadnefs—but despair. 14

SONNET IX.

BLEST is yon shepherd, on the turf reclin'd,
    Who, on the varied clouds which float above,
Lies idly gazing—while his vacant mind
    Pours out some tale antique of rural love!
Ah! *he* has never felt the pangs that move
Th' indignant spirit, when with selfish pride,
Friends, on whose faith the trusting heart rely'd,
    Unkindly shun th' imploring eye of woe!
The ills they ought to soothe, with taunts deride,
    And laugh at tears themselves have forc'd to flow. 10
Nor *his* rude bosom those fine feelings melt,
    Children of Sentiment and Knowledge born,
Thro' whom each shaft with cruel force is felt
    Empoison'd by deceit—or barb'd with scorn.

SONNET X.

To Mrs. G***.

AH! Why will Memory with officious care
   The long lost visions of my days renew!
Why paint the vernal landscape green and fair,
   When life's gay dawn was opening to my view!
Ah! Wherefore bring those moments of delight,
   When with my Anna, on the southern shore,
I thought the future as the present bright!
   Ye dear delusions!—ye return no more!
Alas! How diff'rent does the truth appear,
   From the warm picture youth's rash hand pourtrays!
How fades the scene, as we approach it near,
   And pain and sorrow strike—how many ways!
Yet of that tender heart, ah! still retain
A share for me—and I will not complain!

SONNET XI.

To Sleep.

COME balmy Sleep! tir'd Nature's soft resort!
On these sad temples all thy poppies shed;
And bid gay dreams from Morpheus' airy court,
Float in light vision round my aching head '
Secure of all thy blefsings, partial Power!
On his hard bed the peasant throws him down,
And the poor sea boy, in the rudest hour,   7
Enjoys thee more than he who wears a crown.
Clasp'd in her faithful shepherd's guardian arms,
Well may the village girl sweet slumbers prove;
And they, O gentle Sleep! still taste thy charms,
Who wake to labour, liberty and love.
But still thy opiate aid dost thou deny
To calm the anxious breast; to close the streaming eye.

SONNET XII.

Written on the Sea Shore.—October, 1784.

ON some rude fragment of the rocky shore,
   Where on the fractur'd cliff, the billows break,
   Musing, my solitary seat I take,
And listen to the deep and solemn roar.

O'er the dark waves the winds tempestuous howl ;
   The screaming sea bird quits the troubled sea :
   But the wild gloomy scene has charms for me,
And suits the mournful temper of my soul. 8

Already shipwreck'd by the storms of Fate,
   Like the poor mariner methinks I stand,
   Cast on a rock ; who sees the distant land,
From whence no succour comes, or comes too late.
   Faint and more faint are heard his feeble cries,
   'Till in the rising tide, th' exhausted sufferer dies.

Seymour Sc.

On some rude fragment of the rocky shore

SONNET XIII.

From Petrarch.

Oh ! place me where the burning noon
   Forbids the wither'd flow'r to blow ;
Or place me in the frigid zone,
   On mountains of eternal snow :
Let me pursue the steps of Fame,
   Or Poverty's more tranquil road ;
Let youth's warm tide my veins inflame,
   Or sixty winters chill my blood :
Tho' my fond soul to Heav'n were flown,
   Or tho' on Earth 'tis doom'd to pine,
Prisoner or free—obscure or known,
   My heart, oh Laura ! still is thine.
Whate'er my destiny may be,
That faithful heart, still burns for thee !

SONNET XIV.

From Petrarch.

————————

LOOSE to the wind her golden treffes stream'd, 1
   Forming bright waves, with amorous Zephyr's sighs
   And tho' averted now, her charming eyes
Then with warm love, and melting pity beam'd.
Was I deceiv'd?—Ah! surely, nymph divine!
   That fine suffusion on thy cheek, was love;
   What wonder then those beauteous tints should move
Should fire this heart, this tender heart of mine!
Thy soft melodious voice, thy air, thy shape,
   Were of a goddefs—not a mortal maid;
   Yet tho' thy charms, thy heav'nly charms should fade
My heart, my tender heart could not escape;
   Nor cure for me in time or change be found:
   The shaft extracted, does not cure the wound!

————————

SONNET XV.

From Petrarch.

WHERE the green leaves exclude the summer beam,
  And softly bend as balmy breezes blow,
And where, with liquid lapse, the lucid stream
  Acrofs the fretted rock is heard to flow,
Pensive I lay : When she whom Earth conceals,
  As if still living, to my eyes appears,
And pitying Heaven her angel form reveals,
  To say—' Unhappy Petrarch, dry your tears ;
' Ah ! Why sad lover ! thus before your time,
  ' In grief and sadnefs should your life decay,
' And like a blighted flow'r, your manly prime
  ' In vain and hopelefs sorrow, fade away ?
' Ah ! Yield not thus to culpable despair,
' But raise thine eyes to Heav'n—and think I wait
    thee there.'

SONNET XVI.

From Petrarch.

YE vales and woods! fair scenes of happier hours!
   Ye feather'd people, tenants of the grove !
And you, bright stream! befring'd with shrubs and flow'rs
   Behold my grief, ye witnefses of love !

For ye beheld my infant pafsion rise,
   And saw thro' years unchang'd my faithful flame;
Now cold, in dust, the beauteous object lies,
   And you, ye conscious scenes, are still the same!

While busy memory still delights to dwell
   On all the charms these bitter tears deplore,
And with a trembling hand describes too well
   The angel form I shall behold no more !
To Heaven she's fled ! and nought to me remains
But the pale ashes, which her urn contains.

SONNET XVII.

From the thirteenth Cantata of Metastasio.

ON thy gray bark, in witnefs of my flame,
 I carve Miranda's cypher—beauteous tree !
Grac'd with the lovely letters of her name,
 Henceforth be sacred to my love and me !
Tho' the tall elm, the oak and darker pine,
 With broader arms, may noon's fierce ardors break,
To shelter me, and her I love, be thine ;
 And thine to see her smile and hear her speak.
No bird, ill omen'd, round thy graceful head
 Shall clamour harsh, or wave his heavy wing,
But fern and flow'rs arise beneath thy shade,
 Where the wild bees, their lullabies shall sing,
And in thy boughs the murmuring ringdove rest;
And there the nightingale shall build her nest.

D

SONNET XVIII.

To the Earl of Egremont.

WYNDHAM! 'tis not thy blood, tho' pure it runs
    Thro' a long line of glorious ancestry,
Percys and Seymours, Britain's boasted sons,
    Who trust the honors of their race to thee :

'Tis not thy splendid domes, where science loves
    To touch the canvas, and the bust to raise ;
Thy rich domains, fair fields and spreading groves ;
    'Tis not all these the Muse delights to praise !

In birth, and wealth and honors, great thou art !
    But nobler, in thy independent mind ;
And in that liberal hand and feeling heart
    Giv'n thee by Heav'n—a blefsing to mankind !
Unworthy oft may titled fortune be ;
A soul like thine—is true Nobility !

SONNET XIX.

To Mr. Hayley.

On receiving some elegant Lines from him.

FOR me the Muse a simple band design'd
    Of ' idle' flow'rs, that bloom the woods among,
Which with the cypress and the willow join'd,
    A garland form'd, as artless as my song :
And little dar'd I hope its transient hours
    So long would last ; compos'd of buds so brief ;
'Till Hayley's hand among the vagrant flow'rs,
    Threw from his verdant crown, a deathless leaf.
For high in Fame's bright fane has Judgment plac'd
    The laurel wreath Serena's poet won ;
Which, wov'n with myrtles by the hands of Taste,
    The Muse decreed, for this her favourite son.
And those immortal leaves his temples shade,
Whose fair eternal verdure—shall not fade !

SONNET XX.

To the Countess of A****.

Written on the Anniversary of her Marriage.

ON this blest day may no dark cloud or show'r,
   With envious shade, the Sun's bright influence hide;
But all his rays illume the favour'd hour,
   That saw thee, Mary!—Henry's lovely bride!

With years revolving may it still arise,
   Blest with each good approving Heav'n can lend!
And still with ray serene, shall those blue eyes
   Enchant the husband, and attach the friend!

For you, fair Friendship's amaranth shall blow,
   And Love's own thornless roses, bind your brow!
And when, long hence, to happier worlds you go,
   Your beauteous race shall be, what you are now!
And future Nevills thro' long ages shine,
With hearts as good, and forms as fair as thine!

SONNET XXI.

Suppofed to be written by Werter,

_____

Go! cruel tyrant of the human breaft!

  To other hearts, thy burning arrows bear;

Go, where fond Hope, and fair Illufion reft!

  Ah! Why fhould love inhabit with defpair!

Like the poor maniac I linger here,   5

  Still haunt the fcene, where all my treafure lies,

Still feek for flow'rs, where only thorns appear,

  ' And drink delicious poifon from her eyes!' 8

Tow'rds the deep gulph that opens on my fight

  I hurry forward, Pafsion's helplefs flave!

And fcorning Reafon's mild and fober light,

  Purfue the path that leads me to the grave!

So round the flame the giddy infect flies,

And courts the fatal fire, by which it dies!

_____

D 2

SONNET XXII.

By the fame.

To Solitude.

OH, Solitude ; to thy sequefter'd vale   1

    I come to hide my sorrow and my tears,

And to thy echoes tell the mournful tale

    Which scarce I trust to pitying Friendship's ears !

Amidst thy wild woods, and untrodden glades,

    No sounds but those of melancholy move ;

And the low winds that die among thy shades,

    Seem like soft Pity's sighs, for hope efs love !

And sure some story of despair and pain,

    In yon deep copse, thy murm'ring doves relate ;

And hark ! methinks in that long plaintive strain,

    Thine own sweet songstrefs weeps my wayward fate.

Ah, Nymph ! that fate afsist me to endure,

    And bear awhile—what Death alone can cure !

SONNET XXIII.

By the fame.

To the North Star.

TO thy bright beams I turn my swimming eyes,
  Fair, fav'rite planet ! which in happier days
Saw my young hopes, ah ! faithlefs hopes !—arife ;
  And on my pafsion shed propitious rays !
Now nightly wandering mid the tempests drear
  That howl the woods, and rocky steeps among,
I love to see thy sudden light appear
  Thro' the swift clouds, driv'n by the wind along :
Or in the turbid water, rude and dark,
  O'er whose wild stream the gust of Winter raves,
Thy trembling light with pleasure still I mark,
  Gleam in faint radiance on the foaming waves !
So o'er my soul short rays of reason fly,
Then fade :—and leave me, to despair and die !

SONNET XXIV.

By the fame,

MAKE there my tomb beneath the lime trees' shade,
   Where grafs and flow'rs, in wild luxuriance wave;
Let no memorial mark where I am laid,
   Or point to common eyes the lover's grave!
But oft at twilight morn, or closing day,
   The faithful friend, with fault'ring step shall glide,
Tributes of fond regret by stealth to pay,
   And sigh o'er the unhappy suicide!
And sometimes, when the Sun with parting rays
   Gilds the long grafs that hides my silent bed,
The tear shall tremble in my CHARLOTTE's eyes;
   Dear, precious drops! they shall embalm the dead;
Yes! CHARLOTTE o'er the mournful spot shall weep,
   Where her poor WERTER, and his sorrows--sleep.

SONNET XXV.

By the fame.

Iuſt before his Death.

————————

WHY should I wish to hold in this low sphere 1
   'A frail and feverish being?' wherefore try
Poorly from day to day to linger here,
   Against the powerful hand of Destiny?
By those who know the force of hopeleſs care,
   On the worn heart—I ſure shall be forgıv'n,
If to elude dark guilt, and dire despair,
   I go uncall'd—to mercy and to Heav'n!
Oh thou! to save whose peace I now depart,
   Will thy soft mind, thy poor lost friend deplore,
When worms shall feed on this devoted heart, 11
   Where e'en thy image shall be found no more?
Yet may thy pity mingle not with pain,
For then thy hapleſs lover—dies in vain!

————————

SONNET XXVI.

To the River Arun.

ON thy wild banks, by frequent torrents worn,
 No glittering fanes, or marble domes appear,
Yet shall the mournful muse thy course adorn,
 And still to her thy rustic waves be dear.
For with the infant Otway, lingering here, 5
 Of early woes she bade her vot'ry dream,
While thy low murmurs sooth'd his pensive ear,
 And still the poet—consecrates the stream.
Beneath the oak and birch, that fringe thy side,
 The firstborn violets of the year shall spring,
And in thy hazles, bending o'er the tide,
 The earliest nightingale delight to sing :
While kindred spirits, pitying, shall relate
Thy Otway's sorrows, and lament his fate !

For with the infant Otway lingering here

SONNET XXVII.

SIGHING I see yon little troop at play ;
   By sorrow yet untouch'd ; unhurt by care ;
While free and sportive they enjoy today,
   ' Content and carelefs of tomorrow's fare !' 4
O happy age ! when Hope's unclouded ray
   Lights their green path, and prompts their simple mirth,
Ere yet they feel the thorns that lurking lay
   To wound the wretched pilgrims of the earth,
Making them rue the hour that gave them birth,
   And threw them on a world so full of pain,
Where prosperous Folly treads on patient Worth,
   And to deaf Pride, Misfortune pleads in vain !
Ah !—for their future fate how many fears
Opprefs my heart—and fill mine eyes with tears !

SONNET XXVIII.

To Friendship.

OH thou! whose name too often is profan'd!

　　Whose charms, celestial! few have hearts to feel!

Unknown to Folly—and by Pride disdain'd!

　　—To thy soft solace may my sorrows steal!

Like the fair Moon, thy mild and genuine ray,

　　Thro' life's long evening shall unclouded last;

While Pleasure's frail attachments fleet away,

　　As fades the rainbow from the northern blast!

Tis thine, oh Nymph! with 'balmy hands to bind' 9

　　The wounds inflicted in Misfortune's storm,

　　And blunt severe Affliction's sharpest dart!

—'Tis thy pure spirit warms my Anna's mind,

Beams thro' the pensive softnefs of her form,

　　And holds its altar—on her spotlefs heart!

SONNET XXIX.

To Miss C****.

On being defired to attempt writing a Comedy.

WOULD'ST thou then have *me* tempt the comic scene
   Of gay Thalia ? Us'd so long to tread
   The gloomy paths of Sorrow's cyprefs shade ;
And the lorn lay, with sighs and tears to stain ?
Alas ! how much unfit her sprightly vein !
   Arduous to try !—and seek the sunny mead,
   And bow'rs of roses, where she loves to lead
The sportive subjects of her golden reign !
Enough for me, if still, to soothe my days,
   Her fair and pensive sister condescend,
With tearful smile, to blefs my simple lays ;
   Enough, if her soft notes she sometimes lend,
To gain for me, of feeling hearts the praise,
   And chiefly thine, my ever partial friend !

SONNET XXX.

To the River Arun.

BE the proud Thames, of trade the busy mart!
    Arun! to thee will other praise belong;
Dear to the lover's and the mourner's heart,
    And ever sacred to the Sons of Song!

Thy banks romantic, hopelefs Love shall seek,
    Where o'er the rocks the mantling bindwith flaunts,⁶
And Sorrow's drooping form and faded cheek,
    Choose on thy willow'd shore her lonely haunts!

Banks! which inspir'd thy Otway's plaintive strain!⁹
    Wilds! whose lorn echoes learn'd the deeper tone
Of Collins' pow'rful shell! yet once again
    Another poet—Hayley, is thine own!
Thy clafsic stream anew shall hear a lay,
Bright as its waves, and various as its way!

SONNET XXXI.

Written on Farm Wood, South Downs, May, 1784.

SPRING's dewy hand on this fair summit weaves
 The downy grass, with tufts of Alpine flow'rs,
And shades the beechen slopes with tender leaves,
 And leads the shepherd to his upland bow'rs,
Strewn with wild thyme ; while slow descending show'rs,
 Feed the green ear, and nurse the future sheaves !
—Ah! blest the hind, whom no sad thought bereaves
Of the gay Season's pleasures !—All his hours
To wholesome labour giv'n, or thoughtless mirth ;
 No pangs of sorrow past, or coming dread,
Bend his unconscious spirit down to earth,
 Or chase calm slumbers from his careless head !
Ah ! What to me can those dear days restore,
 When scenes could charm, that now I taste no more !

SONNET XXXII.

To Melancholy.

Written on the Banks of the Arun, October, 1785.

WHEN latest Autumn spreads her evening veil
   And the gray mists from these dim waves arise,
   I love to listen to the hollow sighs,
Thro' the half leafless wood that breathes the gale.
For at such hours the shadowy phantom, pale,
   Oft seems to fleet before the poet's eyes ;
   Strange sounds are heard, and mournful melodies,
As of night wand'rers, who their woes bewail !
Here, by his native stream, at such an hour,
   Pity's own Otway, I methinks could meet,
    And hear his deep sighs swell the sadden'd wind!
Oh Melancholy !—such thy magic power,
   That to the soul these dreams are often sweet,
   And soothe the pensive visionary mind !

SONNET XXXIII.

To the Naiad of the Arun.

Go ! rural Naiad ; wind thy stream along
   Thro' woods and wilds ; then seek the ocean caves
Where sea nymphs meet, their coral rocks among,
   To boast the various honors of their waves !
'Tis but a little, o'er thy shallow tide,
   That toiling Trade her burthen'd vessel leads ;
But laurels grow luxuriant on thy side,
   And letters live, along thy classic meads.
Lo ! where 'mid British bards thy natives shine ! 9
   And now another poet helps to raise
Thy glory high—the poet of the MINE !
   Whose brilliant talents are his smallest praise :
And who, to all that genius can impart,
Adds the cool head, and the unblemish'd heart !

E 2

SONNET XXXIV.

To a Friend.

CHARM'D by thy suffrage, shall I yet aspire,
　　(All inauspicious as my fate appears,
　　By troubles darken'd, that increase with years,)
To guide the crayon, or to touch the lyre ?
Ah me !—the sister Muses still require
　　A spirit free from all intrusive fears,
　　Nor will they deign to wipe away the tears
Of vain regret, that dim their sacred fire.
But when thy envied sanction crowns my lays,
　　A ray of pleasure lights my languid mind,
For well I know the value of thy praise ;
　　And to how few, the flatt'ring meed confin'd,
　　That thou, their highly favour'd brows to bind,
Wilt weave green myrtle and unfading bays !

SONNET XXXV.

To Fortitude.

NYMPH of the rock! whose dauntlefs spirit braves

The beating storm, and bitter winds that howl

Round thy cold breaft; and hear'ft the bursting waves,

And the deep thunder with unshaken soul;

Oh come! and shew how vain the caies that prefs

On my weak bosom—and how little worth

Is the false fleeting meteor, Happinefs,

That still misleads the wand'rers of the earth!

Strengthen'd by thee, this heart shall cease to melt

O'er ills that poor Humanity muft bear;

Nor friends estrang'd, or ties difsolv'd be felt

To leave regret, and fruitlefs anguish there:

And when at length it heaves its latest sigh,

Thou, and mild Hope, shall teach me how to die!

SONNET XXXVI.

SHOULD the lone Wand'rer, fainting on his way,

Rest for a moment of the sultry hours,

And tho' his path thro' thorns and roughnefs lay,

Pluck the wild rose, or woodbine's gadding flow'rs;

Weaving gay wreaths, beneath some shelt'ring tree,

The sense of sorrow, he awhile may lose;

So have I sought thy flow'rs, fair Poesy!

So charm'd my way, with Friendship and the Muse.

But darker now grows Life's unhappy day,

Dark, with new clouds of evil yet to come,

Her pencil sickening Fancy throws away,

And weary Hope reclines upon the tomb;

And points my wishes to that tranquil shore,

Where the pale spectre Care, pursues no more.

Seymour sc.

Her pencil sickening fancy throws away
And weary hope reclines upon the tomb.

SONNET XXXVII.

Sent to the Hon. Mrs. O'Niell, with painted Flowers.

——

THE poet's fancy takes from Flora's realm
   Her buds and leaves to drefs fictitious powers,
With the green olive shades Minerva's helm,
   And gives to Beauty's Queen, the Queen of Flowers.
But what gay bloſsoms of luxuriant Spring,
   With rose, mimosa, amaranth entwin'd,
Shall fabled Sylphs, and fairy people bring,
   As a juſt emblem of the lovely mind?
In vain the mimic pencil tries to blend
   The glowing dyes that drefs the flow'ry race,
   Scented and colour'd by a hand divine!
Ah! not lefs vainly would the Muse pretend
   On her weak lyre, to sing the native grace
   And native goodnefs of a soul like thine!

——

SONNET XXXVIII.

From the Novel of Emmeline.

WHEN welcome slumber sets my spirit free,
　　Forth to fictitious happiness it flies,
　　And where Elysian bow'rs of blifs arise
I seem, my Emmeline—to meet with thee !
Ah ! Fancy then, difsolving human ties,
　　Gives me the wishes of my soul to see ;
Tears of fond pity fill thy soften'd eyes ;
　　In heav'nly harmony—our hearts agree.
Alas ! these joys are mine in dreams alone,
When cruel Reason abdicates her throne !
　　Her harsh return condemns me to complain
Thro' life unpitied, unreliev'd, unknown.
　　And as the dear delusions leave my brain,
　　She bids the truth recur—with aggravated pain.

SONNET XXXIX.

To Night.

From the same.

I LOVE thee, mournful, sobersuited night,
　　When the faint moon, yet ling'ring in her wane,
And veil'd in clouds, with pale uncertain light
　　Hangs o'er the waters of the restless main.
In deep depression sunk, th' enfeebled mind
　　Will to the deaf, cold elements complain,
　　And tell th' embosom'd grief, however vain,
To sullen surges and the viewless wind.
Tho' no repose on thy dark breast I find,
　　I still enjoy thee—cheerless as thou art;
　　For in thy quiet gloom, th' exhausted heart
Is calm, tho' wretched; hopeless, yet resign'd.
　　While, to the winds and waves its sorrows giv'n,
　　May reach—tho' lost on earth—the ear of Heav'n!

SONNET XL.

From the fame.

FAR on the sands, the low, etiring tide,
   In distant murmurs hardly seems to flow,
And o'er the world of waters, blue and wide,
   The sighing summer wind forgets to blow.
As sinks the daystar in the rosy West,
   The silent wave, with rich reflection glows ;
Alas ! Can tranquil Nature give *me* rest,
   Or scenes of beauty, soothe me to repose ?
Can the soft lustre of the sleeping main,
   Yon radiant Heaven, or all Creation's charms,
' Erase the written troubles of the brain,'
   Which Memory tortures, and which Guilt alarms ?
Or bid a bosom transient quiet prove,
That bleeds with vain remorse, and unextinguish'd love !

SONNET XLI.

To Tranquillity.

IN this tumultuous sphere, for thee unfit,
　　How seldom art thou found—Tranquillity !
　　Unlefs 'tis when with mild and downcast eye,
By the low cradles, thou delight'st to sit,
Of sleeping infants—watching the soft breath,
　　And bidding the sweet slumb'rers easy lie ;
Or sometimes hanging o'er the bed of death,
　　Where the poor languid suff'rer—hopes to die,
Oh ! beauteous sister of the halcyon Peace !
　　I sure shall find thee in that heav'nly scene
　　　Where Care and Anguish shall their pow'r resign ;
Where Hope alike, and vain Regret shall cease ;
　　And Memory—lost in happinefs serene,
　　　Repeat no more—that misery has been mine !

SONNET XLII.

Composed during a Walk on the Downs, Nov. 1787.

THE dark and pillowy cloud; the sallow trees,

Seem o'er the ruins of the year to mourn ;

And cold and hollow, the inconstant breeze

Sobs thro' the falling leaves and wither'd fern.

O'er the tall brow of yonder chalky bourn,

The evening shades their gather'd darkness fling,

While, by the ling'ring light, I scarce discern

The shrieking nightjar, sail on heavy wing. 8

Ah! yet a little—and propitious Spring,

Crown'd with fresh flow'rs, shall wake the woodland strain;

But no gay change revolving seasons bring,

To call forth Pleasure from the soul of Pain,

Bid syren Hope resume her long lost part,

And chase the vulture Care, that feeds upon the heart.

SONNET XLIII.

THE unhappy exile, whom his fates confine
  To the bleak coast of some unfriendly isle,
  Cold, barren, desert, where no harvests smile,
But thirst and hunger on the rocks repine ;
When, from some promontory's fearful brow,
  Sun after sun he hopeless sees decline
In the broad shipless sea—perhaps may know
  Such heartless pain, such blank despair as mine ;
And, if a flatt'ring cloud appears to show
  The fancied semblance of a distant sail,
  Then melts away—anew his spirits fail,
While the lost hope but aggravates his woe !
Ah ! so for me delusive Fancy toils,
Then, from contrasted truth—my feeble soul recoils

SONNET XLIV.

Written in the Church Yard at Middleton in Sussex.

PRESS'D by the Moon, mute arbitrefs of tides,
 While the loud equinox its pow'r combines,
 The sea no more its swelling surge confines,
But o'er the shrinking land sublimely rides.
The wild blasts, rising from the western cave,
 Drives the huge billows from their heaving bed;
 Tears from their grafsy tombs the village dead, 7
And breaks the silent sabbath of the grave!
With shells and seaweed mingled, on the shore,
 Lo! their bones whiten in the frequent wave;
 But vain to them the winds and waters rave;
They hear the warring elements no more:
While I am doom'd—by life's long storm opprest,
To gaze with envy, on their gloomy rest.

SONNET XLV.

On leaving a part of Sussex.

FAREWELL Aruna!—on whose varied shore
  My early vows were paid to Nature's shrine,
  When thoughtlefs Joy, and infant Hope were mine,
And whose lorn stream has heard me since deplore
  Too many sorrows! Sighing I resign
Thy solitary beauties—and no more,
  Or on thy rocks, or in thy woods recline,
Or on the heath, by moonlight ling'ring, pore
  On air drawn phantoms—While in Fancy's ear
As in the evening wind thy murmurs swell,
  Th' Enthusiast of the Lyre, who wander'd here, 11
Seems yet to strike his visionary shell,
  Of power to call forth Pity's tend'rest tear,
Or wake wild Frenzy—from her hideous cell!

F 2

SONNET XLVI.

Written at Penshurst, in Autumn, 1788.

YE Tow'rs sublime, deserted now and drear,
　Ye woods, deep sighing to the hollow blast,
The musing wand'rer loves to linger near,
　While History points to all your glories past :
And startling from their haunts the timid deer,
　To trace the walks obscur'd by matted fern,
Which Waller's soothing lyre were wont to hear,
　But where now clamours the discordant hern ! 8
The spoiling hand of Time may overturn
　These lofty battlements, and quite deface
The fading canvas whence we love to learn
　Sydney's keen look, and Sacharifsa's grace ;
But Fame and Beauty still defy decay,
Sav'd by th' historic page—the poet's tender lay !

SONNET XLVII.

To Fancy.

THEE, Queen of Shadows!—shall I still invoke,
  Still love the scenes thy sportive pencil drew,
When on mine eyes the early radiance broke
  Which shew'd the beauteous, rather than the true!
Alas! long since, those glowing tints are dead,
  And now 'tis thine in darkest hues to drefs
The spot where pale Experience hangs her head
  O'er the sad grave of murder'd Happinefs!
Thro' thy false medium then, no longer view'd,
  May fancied pain and fancied pleasure fly,
    And I, as from me all thy dreams depart,
Be to my wayward destiny subdu'd;
  Nor seek perfection with a poet's eye,
    Nor suffer anguish with a poet's heart!

SONNET XLVIII.

To 𝔐𝔯𝔰. ****.

No more my wearied soul attempts to stray
   From sad Reality and vain Regret,
Nor courts enchanting Fiction to allay
   Sorrows that Sense refuses to forget :
For of Calamity so long the prey,
   Imagination now has lost her pow'rs,
Nor will her fairy loom again efsay
   To drefs Affliction in a robe of flow'rs.
But if no more the bow'rs of Fancy bloom,
   Let one superior scene attract my view,
Where Heav'n's pure rays the sacred spot illume,
   Let *thy* lov'd hand with palm and am'ranth strew
The mournful path approaching to the tomb,
While Faith's consoling voice endears the friendly gloom.

SONNET XLIX.

Supposed to have been written in a Church Yard, over the Grave of a young Woman of nineteen.

From the Novel of Celestina.

OH, thou ! who sleep'st where hazle bands entwine
  The vernal grafs, with paler violets drest ;
I would, sweet maid ! thy humble bed were mine,
  And mine thy calm and enviable rest.
For never more by human ills opprest,
  Shall thy soft spirit fruitlefsly repine :
  Thou canst not now, thy fondest hopes resign
E'en in the hour that should have made thee blest.
Light lies the turf upon thy virgin breast ;
  And ling'ring here, to Love and Sorrow true,
The Youth who once thy simple heart pofsest
  Shall mingle tears with April's early dew ;
While still for him shall faithful Memory save
Thy form and virtues from the silent grave.

SONNET L.

From the Novel of Celestina.

FAREWELL, ye lawns! by fond Remembrance blest,
As witnesses of gay unclouded hours;
Where, to maternal Friendship's bosom prest,
My happy childhood past amid your bow'rs.
Ye woodwalks wild!—where leaves and fairy flow'n
By Spring's luxuriant hand are strewn anew;
Rocks! whence with shadowy grace rude Nature low'r
O'er glens and haunted streams!—a long adieu!
And you!—oh promis'd Happiness!—whose voice
Deluded Fancy heard in ev'ry grove,
Bidding this tender, trusting heart rejoice
In the bright prospect of unfailing love:
Tho' lost to me—still may thy smile serene
Bless the dear lord—of this regretted scene.

SONNET LI.

Suppoſed to have been written in the Hebrides.

From the Novel of Celeſtina.

ON this lone island, whose unfruitful breast
   Feeds but the summer shepherd's little flock,
   With scanty herbage from the half cloth'd rock
Where osprays, cormorants and seamews rest; 4
   E'en in a scene so desolate and rude
I could with *thee* for months and years be blest;
And, of thy tenderneſs and love poſsest,
   Find all *my* world in this wild solitude !
When Summer suns these northern seas illume,
   With thee admire the light's reflected charms,
And when drear Winter spreads his cheerleſs gloom,
   Still find Elysium in thy shelt'ring arms :
For thou to me canst sov'reign bliſs impart,
Thy mind my empire—and my throne thy heart.

SONNET LII.

The Pilgrim.

From the Novel of Celestina.

FAULT'RING and sad, th' unhappy Pilgrim roves,
   Who, on the eve of bleak December's night,
Divided far from all he fondly loves,
   Journeys alone, along the giddy height
Of these steep cliffs, and as the sun's last ray
   Fades in the west, sees, from the rocky verge,
Dark tempest scowling o'er the shorten'd day,
   And hears with ear appall'd, th' impetuous surge
Beneath him thunder!—So, with heart opprefs'd,
   Alone, reluctant, desolate and slow,
By Friendship's cheering radiance *now* unblest,
   Along Life's rudest path I seem to go;
Nor see where yet the anxious heart may rest,
   That trembling at the past—recoils from future woe

SONNET LIII.

The Laplander.

From the Novel of Celeflina.

THE shiv'ring native, who by Tenglio's side
  Beholds, with fond regret, the parting light
Sink far away, beneath the dark'ning tide,
  And leave him to long months of dreary night;
Yet knows, that springing from the eastern wave,
  The sun's glad beams shall reillume his way,
And from the snows secur'd—within his cave
  He waits, in patient hope—returning day.
Not so the suff'rer feels, who, o'er the waste
  Of joylefs life, is destin'd to deplore
Fond love forgotten, tender friendship past,
  Which, once extinguish'd, can revive no more!
O'er the blank void, he looks with hopelefs pain;
For him those beams of Heaven, shall never shine again.

G

SONNET LIV.

The sleeping Woodman.

Written in April, 1790.

YE copses wild, where April bids arise
    The vernal grafses, and the early flow'rs ;
My soul deprefs'd—from human converse fies
    To the lone shelter of your pathlefs bow'rs.
Lo!—where the Woodman, with his toil opprefs'd,
    His carelefs head, on bark and mofs reclin'd,
    Lull'd by the song of birds, the murm'ring wind,
Has sunk to calm, tho' momentary, rest.
Ah! would 'twere mine in Spring's green lap to find
    Such transient respite from the ills I bear !
Would I could taste, like this unthinking hind,
    A sweet forgetfulnefs of human care, 12
'Till the last sleep these weary eyes shall close,
And Death receive me to his long repose,

SONNET LV.

The Return of the Nightingale.

Written in May, 1791

BORNE on the warm wing of the western gale,
   How tremulously low is heard to float,
Thro' the green budding thorns that fringe the vale,
   The early Nightingale's prelusive note.
'Tis Hope's instinctive pow'r that, thro' the grove,
   Tells how benignant Heav'n revives the earth,
'Tis the soft voice of young and timid love
   That calls these melting sounds of sweetness forth
With transport, once, sweet bird! I hail'd thy lay,
   And bade thee welcome to our shades again,
To charm the wand'ring poet's pensive way,
   And soothe the solitary lover's pain;
But now!—such evils in my lot combine,
As shut my languid sense, to Hope's dear voice and thine.

SONNET LVI.

The Captive escaped in the Wilds of America.

Addressed to the Honourable Mrs. O'Neill.

If by his torturing, savage foes untrac'd,
   The breathless Captive gain some trackless glade,
Yet hears the warwhoop howl along the waste,
   And dreads the reptile monsters of the shade ;
The giant reeds that murmur round the flood,
   Seem to conceal some hideous form beneath ;
And every hollow blast that shakes the wood,
   Speaks to his trembling heart, of woe and death.
With horror fraught, and desolate dismay,
   On such a wanderer falls the starless night ;
But if, far streaming, a propitious ray
   Leads to some amicable fort his sight,
He hails the beam benign that guides his way,
   As I, my Harriet, bless thy friendship's cheering light.

SONNET LVII.

To Dependence.

DEPENDENCE! heavy, heavy are thy chains,
  And happier they, who from the dangerous sea,
Or the dark mine, procure with ceaseless pains
  A hard earn'd pittance—than who trust to thee!
More blest the hind, who, from his bed of flock
  Starts! when the birds of morn their summons give,
And waken'd by the lark, ' the shepherd's clock', 7
  Lives but to labour—labouring but to live
More noble than the sycophant, whose art
  Must heap with taudry flow'rs thy hated shrine,
I envy not the meed thou canst impart
  To crown *his* service—while, tho' Pride combine
With Fraud to crush me—my unfetter'd heart
  Still to the Mountain Nymph may offer mine. 14

G 2

SONNET LVIII.

The Glow Worm.

WHEN, on some balmy breathing night of Spring,
 The happy child, to whom the world is new,
Pursues the evening moth, of mealy wing,
 Or from the heathbell beats the sparkling dew ;
He sees before his inexperienc'd eyes,
 The brilliant Glow Worm, like a meteor, shine
On the turf bank ;—amaz'd and pleas'd he cries
 ' Star of the dewy grafs !—I make thee mine !' 8
Then, ere he sleep, collects 'the moisten'd' flow'r, 9
 And bids soft leaves his glittering prize enfold,
And dreams that fairy lamps illume his bow'r :
 Yet with the morning, shudders to behold
His lucid treasure, raylefs as the dust ;
 So turn the world's bright joys, to cold and blank disgust.

SONNET LIX.

Written during a Thunder Storm,

September, 1791; in which the Moon was perfectly clear, while the Tempest gathered in various directions near the Earth.

WHAT awful pageants croud the evening sky!
The low horizon gath'ring vapours shroud,
    Sudden, from many a deep embattled cloud,
Terrific thunders burst and light'nings fly—
While in serenest azure, beaming high,
    Night's regent—of her calm pavilion proud;
Gilds the dark shadows that beneath her lie,
    Unvex'd by all their conflicts fierce and loud—
So, in unsullied dignity elate,
    A spirit conscious of superior worth,
In placid elevation firmly great,
    Scorns the vain cares that give Contention birth ;
And blest with peace above the shocks of Fate,
    Smiles at the tumult of the troubled earth.

Ode to Despair.

From the Novel of Emmeline.

THOU spectre of terrific mein,

   Lord of the hopeless heart and hollow eye,

In whose fierce train each form is seen

   That drives sick Reason to insanity!

    I woo thee with unusual pray'r,

    ' Grim visag'd, comfortless Despair !'

Approach ; in me a willing victim find,

Who seeks thine iron sway—and calls thee kind !

Ah ! hide forever from my sight

   The faithless flatt'rer Hope—whose pencil, gay,

Pourtrays some vision of delight,

   Then bids the fairy tablet fade away ;

    While in dire contrast, to mine eyes

    Thy phantoms, yet more hideous, rise,

                And

And Mem'ry draws, from Pleasure's wither'd flow'r,
Corrosives for the heart—of fatal pow'r !

I bid the traitor Love, adieu !
    Who to this fond, believing bosom came,
A guest insidious and untrue,
    With Pity's soothing voice—in Friendship's name ;
        The wounds *he* gave, nor Time shall cure,
        Nor Reason teach me to endure :
And to that breast mild Patience pleads in vain,
Which feels the curse—of meriting its pain.

Yet not to me, tremendous pow'r !
    Thy worst of spirit wounding pangs impart,
With which, in dark Conviction's hour,
    Thou strik'st the guilty, unrepentant heart !
        But of illusion long the sport,
        That dreary, tranquil gloom I court,
Where my past errors I may still deplore,
And dream of long lost Happiness no more !

To

To thee I give this tortur'd breast,
   Where Hope arises but to foster pain;
Ah! lull its agonies to rest!
   Ah! let me never be deceiv'd again!
     But callous, in thy deep repose
     Behold, in long array, the woes
Of the dread future, calm and undismay'd,
Till I may claim the Hope—that shall not fade!

Elegy. I

'DARK gath'ring clouds involve the threat'ning skies,
   ' The sea heaves conscious of th'impending gloom,
' Deep, hollow murmurs from the cliffs arise ;
   ' They come—the Spirits of the Tempest come !

' Oh! may such terrors mark th' approaching night
   ' As reign'd on that these streaming eyes deplore!
' Flash, ye red fires of Heav'n, with fatal light,
   ' And with conflicting winds, ye waters roar !

Loud, and more loud, ye foaming billows burst!
   ' Ye warring elements more fiercely rave !
' Till the wide waves o'erwhelm the spot accurst,
   " Where ruthless Avarice finds a quiet grave!"

                              Thus

Thus with clasp'd hands, wild looks and streaming hair,
    While shrieks of horror broke her trembling speech,
A wretched maid—the victim of Despair,
    Survey'd the threat'ning storm and desert beech;

Then to the tomb where now the father slept,
    Whose rugged nature bade her sorrows flow,
Frantic she turn'd—and beat her breast and wept,
    Invoking vengeance on the dust below.

' Lo! rising there above each humbler heap,
    ' Yon cypher'd stones *his* name and wealth relate,
' Who gave his son—remorselefs—to the deep,
    ' While I, his living victim, curse my fate.

' Oh! my lost love! no tomb is plac'd for thee,
    ' That may to strangers' eyes thy worth impart;
' Thou hast no grave, but in the stormy sea,
    ' And no memorial, but this breaking heart.

                    ' Forth

' Forth to the world, a widow'd wand'rer driv'n,

   ' I pour to winds and waves th' unheeded tear,

' Try with vain effort to submit to Heav'n,

   ' And fruitlefs call on him—" who cannot hear."

' Oh! might I fondly clasp him once again,

   ' While o'er my head th' infuriate billows pour,

' Forget in Death this agonizing pain,

   ' And feel his father's cruelty no more!

' Part, raging waters, part, and shew beneath,

   ' In your dread caves, his pale and mangled form.

' Now, while the demons of Despair and Death

   ' Ride on the blast, and urge the howling storm!

' Lo! by the light'ning's momentary blaze,

   ' I see him rise the whitening waves above,

No longer such as when in happier days

   ' He gave th' enchanted hours—to me and love.

                          ' Such

U

' Such, as when daring the enchafed sea,

    ' And courting dang'rous toil, he often said,

' That every peril, one soft smile from me,

    ' One sigh of speechless tenderness, o'erpaid.

' But dead, disfigur'd, while between the roar

    ' Of the loud waves his accents pierce mine ear,

' And seem to say—Ah! wretch, delay no more,

    ' But come, unhappy mourner—meet me here.

' Yet, powerful Fancy, bid the phantom stay,

    ' Still let me hear him !—'Tis already past ;

' Along the waves his shadow glides away,

    ' I lose his voice amid the deaf'ning blast.

' Ah! wild Illusion, born of frantic Pain !

    ' He hears not, comes not from his wat'ry bed ;

' My tears, my anguish, my despair are vain,

    ' Th' insatiate ocean gives not up its dead.

                               ' 'Tis

' 'Tis not his voice ! Hark ! the deep thunders roll ;
   ' Up heaves the ground ; the rocky barriers fail ;
' Approach, ye horrors that delight my soul,
   ' Despair, and Death, and Desolation—hail ''

The ocean hears—th' embodied waters come—
   Rise o'er the land, and with resistless sweep
Tear from its base the proud aggressor's tomb,
   And bear the injured to eternal sleep !

Song.

From the French of Cardinal Bernis

I.

FRUIT of Aurora's tears, fair rose,
  On whose soft leaves fond Zephyrs play,
Oh! queen of flow'rs, thy buds disclose,
  And give thy fragrance to the day ;
Unveil thy transient charms :—ah, no!
  A little be thy bloom delay'd,
Since the same hour that bids thee blow
  Shall see thee droop thy languid head.

II.

But go! and on Themira's breast
  Find, happy flow'r, thy throne and tomb ;
While, jealous of a fate so blest,
  How shall I envy thee thy doom!

                              Should

Should some rude hand approach thee there,

    Guard the sweet shrine thou wilt adorn,

Ah! punish those who rashly dare,

    And for my rivals keep thy thorn.

III.

Love shall himself thy boughs compose,

    And bid thy wanton leaves divide;

He'll shew thee how, my lovely rose,

    To deck her bosom, not to hide:

And thou shalt tell the cruel maid

    How frail are Youth and Beauty's charms,

And teach her, ere her own shall fade,

    To give them to her lover's arms.

Origin of Flattery.

WHEN Jove, in anger to the sons of earth,
Bid artful Vulcan give Pandora birth,
And sent the fatal gift, which spread below
O'er all the wretched race, contagious woe,
Unhappy man, by Vice and Folly tost,
Found in the storms of life his quiet lost,
While Envy, Avarice and Ambition, hurl'd
Discord and Death around the warring world ;
Then the blest peasant left his fields and fold,
And barter'd love and peace for pow'r and gold ;
Left his calm cottage and his native plain,
In search of wealth to tempt the faithlefs main ;
Or, braving danger, in the battle stood,
And bath'd his savage hands in human blood :

No

No longer then, his woodland walks among,
The shepherd lad his genuine pafsion sung,
Or sought at early morn his soul's delight,
Or grav'd her name upon the bark at night ;
To deck her flowing hair no more he wove
The simple wreath, or with ambitious love
Bound his own brow with myrtle or with bay,
But broke his pipe, and threw his crook away.
The nymphs forsaken, other pleasures sought ;
Then first for gold their venal hearts were bought,
And Nature's blush to sickly Art gave place,
And Affectation seiz'd the seat of Grace :
No more Simplicity, by Sense refin'd,
Or gen'rous Sentiment, pofsefs'd the mind ;
No more they felt each other's joy and woe,
And Cupid fled, and hid his uselefs bow.
But with deep grief propitious Venus pin'd,
To see the ills which threaten'd womankind ;
Ills, that she knew her empire would disarm,
And rob her subjects of their sweetest charm ;

Good

Good humour's potent influence destroy,

And change for low'ring frowns, the smile of joy.

Then deeply sighing at the mournful view,

She try'd at length what heavenly Art could do

To bring back Pleasure to her pensive train,

And vindicate the glories of her reign.

A thousand little loves attend the task,

And bear from Mars's head his radiant casque,

The fair enchantrefs on its silver bound,

Wreath'd with soft spells her magic cestus round.

Then shaking from her hair ambrosial dew,

Infus'd fair Hope, and Expectation new,

And stifled wishes, and persuasive sighs,

And fond belief, and ' eloquence of eyes,'

And fault'ring accents, which explain so well

What studied speeches vainly try to tell,

And more pathetic silence, which imparts

Infectious tendernefs to feeling hearts,

Soft tones of pity ; fascinating smiles ;

And Maia's son afsisted her with wiles,

And

And brought gay dreams, fantastic visions brought,

And wav'd his wand o'er the seducing draught.

Then Zephyr came: To him the goddess cry'd,

' Go fetch from Flora all her flow'ry pride

' To fill my charm, each scented bud that blows,

' And bind my myrtles with her thornless rose ;

' Then speed thy flight to Gallia's smiling plain,

' Where rolls the Loire, the Garonne and the Seine ;

' Dip in their waters thy celestial wing,

' And the soft dew to fill my chalice bring ;

' But chiefly tell thy Flora, that to me

' She send a bouquet of her fleurs de lys ;

' That poignant spirit will complete my spell.'

—'Tis done I the lovely sorc'ress says 'tis well.

And now Apollo lends a ray of fire,

The caldron bubbles, and the flames aspire ;

The watchful Graces round the circle dance,

With arms entwin'd, to mark the work's advance ;

And with full quiver sportive Cupid came,

Temp'ring his fav'rite arrows in the flame.

Then

Then Venus speaks, the wav'ring flames retire,

And Zephyr's breath extinguishes the fire.

At length the goddefs in the helmet's round

A sweet and subtile spirit duly found,

More soft than oil, than ether more refin'd,

Of pow'r to cure the woes of womankind,

And call'd it Flatt'ry :—balm of female life,

It charms alike the widow, maid and wife ;

Clears the sad brow of virgins in despair,

And smooths the cruel traces left by Care ;

Bids palsy'd Age with youthful spirit glow,

And hangs May's garlands on December's snow.

Delicious efsence ! howsoe'er apply'd,

By what rude nature is thy charm deny'd ?

Some form seducing still thy whisper wears,

Stern Wisdom turns to thee her willing ears,

And Prudery listens, and forgets her fears.

The rustic nymph, whom rigid aunts restrain,

Condemn'd to drefs, and practise airs in vain,

At

At thy first summons finds her bosom swell,

And bids her crabbed governantes farewell ;

While, fir'd by thee with spirit not her own,

She grows a toast, and rises into *ton*.

The faded beauty who with secret pain,

Sees younger charms usurp her envied reign,

By thee afsisted, can with smiles behold

The record where her conquests are enroll'd ;

And dwelling yet on scenes by mem'ry nurs'd,

When George the second reign'd, or George the first ;

She sees the shades of ancient beaux arise,

Who swear her eyes exceeded modern eyes,

When poets sung for her and lovers bled,

And giddy Fashion follow'd as she led.

Departed modes appear in long array,

The flow'rs and flounces of her happier day ;

Again her locks the decent fillets bind,

The waving lappet flutters in the wind,

And then comparing with a proud disdain

The more fantastic tastes that now obtain,

She

She deems ungraceful, trifling and absurd,

The gayer world that moves round George the third

Nor thy soft influence will the train refuse,

Who court in distant shades the modest Muse,

Tho' in a form more pure and more refin'd,

Thy soothing spirit meets the letter'd mind ;

Not Death itself thine empire can destroy ;

Tow'rds thee, e'en then, we turn the languid eye ;

Still trust in thee to bid our mem'ry bloom,

And scatter roses round the silent tomb.

Peasant of the Alps.

From the Novel of Celeftina

WHERE cliffs arise by Winter crown'd,
And through dark groves of pine around,
Down the deep chasms, the snowfed torrents foam,
Within some hollow, shelter'd from the storms,
The PEASANT of the ALPS his cottage forms,
And builds his humble, happy home.

Unenvied is the rich domain,
That far beneath him on the plain,
Waves its wide harvests and its olive groves;
More dear to him his hut, with plantain thatch'd,
Where long his unambitious heart attach'd,
Finds all he wishes, all he loves.

There

There dwells the mistress of his heart,
And *Love* who teaches ev'ry art,
Has bid him dress the spot with fondest care ;
When borrowing from the vale its fertile soil,
He climbs the precipice with patient toil,
To plant her fav'rite flow'rets there.

With native shrubs, a hardy race,
There the green myrtle finds a place,
And roses there, the dewy leaves decline ;
While from the crags' abrupt and tangled steeps,
With bloom and fruit the Alpine berry peeps,
And, blushing, mingles with the vine.

His garden's simple produce stor'd,
Prepar'd for him by hands ador'd,
Is all the little luxury he knows :
And by the same dear hands are softly spread,
The Chamois' velvet spoil that forms the bed,
Where in her arms he finds repose.

But

But absent from the calm abode,
Dark thunder gathers round his road,
Wild raves the wind, the arrowy light'nings flash,
Returning quick the murmuring rocks among,
His faint heart trembling as he winds along ;
Alarm'd!—he listens to the crash

Of rifted ice !—Oh, man of woe !
O'er his dear cot—a mass of snow,
By the storm sever'd from the cliff above,
Has fall'n—and buried in its marble breast,
All that for him—lost wretch—the world possest,
His home, his happiness, his love !

Aghast the heartstruck mourner stands !
Glaz'd are his eyes—convuls'd his hands,
O'erwhelming Anguish checks his labouring breath;
Crush'd by Despair's intolerable weight,
Frantic he seeks the mountain's giddiest height,
And headlong seeks relief in death.

A

A fate too similar is mine,

But I—in ling'ring pain repine,

And still my lost felicity deplore ;

Cold, cold to me is that dear breast become,

Where this poor heart had fondly fix'd its home,

And love and happiness are mine no more.

Song.

DOES Pity give, tho' Fate denies,
   And to my wounds her balm impart :
O speak! with those exprefsive eyes ;
   Let one low sigh escape thine heart.

The gazing croud shall never guefs
   What anxious, watchful love can see ;
Nor know what those soft looks exprefs,
   Nor dream that sigh is meant for me.

Ah! words are uselefs, words are vain,
   Thy gen'rous sympathy to prove ;
And well, that sigh, those looks explain,
   That Clara mourns my haplefs love.

Thirty Eight.

Addressed to Mrs H——y.

IN early youth's unclouded scene,
The brilliant morning of eighteen,
    With health and sprightly joy elate,
We gaz'd on Life's enchanting spring,
Nor thought how quickly Time would bring
    The mournful period—Thirty eight.

Then the starch maid, or matron sage,
Already of that sober age,
    We view'd with mingled scorn and hate;
In whose sharp words or sharper face,
With thoughtless mirth we lov'd to trace
    The sad effects of Thirty eight.

Till

Till sadd'ning, sick'ning at the view,
We learn'd to dread what Time might do;
 And then preferr'd a prayer to Fate,
To end our days ere that arriv'd;
When (pow'r and pleasure long surviv'd)
 We met neglect and—Thirty eight.

But Time, in spite of wishes, flies,
And Fate our simple prayer denies,
 And bids us Death's own hour await:
The auburn locks are mix'd with grey,
The transient roses fade away,
 But Reason comes at—Thirty eight.

Her voice the anguish contradicts
That dying Vanity inflicts;
 Her hand new pleasures can create,
For us she opens to the view
Prospects lefs bright—but far more true,
 And bids us smile at—Thirty eight.

No more shall *Scandal*'s breath destroy

The social converse we enjoy

　　With bard or critic tête a tête ;

O'er Youth's bright blooms her blights shall pour,

But spare th' improving friendly hour

　　That Science gives to—Thirty eight.

Stripp'd of their gaudy hues by Truth,

We view the glitt'ring toys of Youth,

　　And blush to think how poor the bait,

For which to public scenes we ran,

And scorn'd of sober Sense the plan

　　Which gives content at—Thirty eight.

Tho' Time's inexorable sway

Has torn the myrtle bands away,

　　For other wreaths 'tis not too late,

The am'ranth's purple glow survives,

And still Minerva's olive lives

　　On the calm brow of—Thirty eight.

With

With eye more steady we engage

To contemplate approaching age,

And life more justly estimate ;

With firmer souls, and stronger pow'rs,

With Reason, Faith and Friendship ours,

We'll not regret the stealing hours

That lead from Thirty—e'en to Forty eight.

Verses.

Intended to have been prefixed to the Novel of Emmeline, but then
suppressed.

O'ERWHELM'D with Sorrow, and sustaining long,
'The proud man's contumely, the oppressor's wrong,'
Languid Despondency and vain Regret,
Must my exhausted spirit struggle yet?
Yes! robb'd myself, of all that Fortune gave,
E'en of all hope—but shelter in the grave,
Still shall the plaintive lyre essay its pow'rs
To dress the cave of Care, with Fancy's flow'rs,
Maternal Love, the fiend Despair withstand,
Still animate the heart and guide the hand.
—May you, dear objects of my anxious care,
Escape the evils—I was born to bear!
Round my devoted head, while tempests roll,
Yet there, where I have treasur'd up my soul,

May

May the soft rays of dawning Hope impart
Reviving Patience to my fainting heart;
And, when its sharp solicitudes shall cease,
May I be conscious in the realms of Peace
That ev'ry tear which swells my children's eyes,
From sorrows past, not present ills arise.
Then, with some friend who loves to share your pain,
For 'tis my boast that *some* such friends remain,
By filial grief, and fond remembrance prest,
You'll seek the spot, where all my sorrows rest;
Recall my haplefs days in sad review,
The long calamities I bore for you,
And—with a happier fate—resolve to prove
How well you merited—your mother's love.

QUOTATIONS, NOTES and EXPLA-NATIONS.

SONNET I.

LINE 13.

All! then, how dear the Muse's favors cost,
If those paint sorrow best—who feel it most!

The well sung woes shall soothe my pensive ghost;
He best can paint them, who shall feel them most.

Pope's Eloisa to Abelard, 366th line.

SONNET II.

LINE 3.

Anemonies, that spangled every grove.
Anemony Nemeroso.   The wood Anemony.

K   SONNET

SONNET III.

LINE 1.

The idea from the 43d Sonnet of Petrarch. Secondo parte.

Quel rosigniuol, che si soave piagne.

SONNET V.

LINE 2.

Your turf, your flowers among.

Whose turf, whose shades, whose flowers among,

Gray.

LINE 9.

Aruna !

The river Arun.

SONNET VI.

LINE 12.

'For me the vernal garland blooms no more.'

Pope's Imit. 1st Ode 4th Book of Horace.

' Mifery's love.'

Shakespeare's King John.

SONNET VII.

' On the night's dull ear.'

Shakespeare.

Whether on Spring—Alludes to the supposed migration of the Nightingale.

The pensive Muse shall own thee for her mate.

Whether the Muse or Love call thee his mate,
Both them I ferve, and of their train am I.

Milton's First Sonnet.

SONNET

SONNET VIII.

LINE 14.

Have power to cure all sadnefs—but despair !

To the heart inspires
Vernal delight and joy, able to drive
All sadnefs but despair.

Paradise Lost, Fourth Book.

SONNET IX.

LINE 10.

And laugh at tears themselves have forc'd to flow.

And hard Unkindnefs' alter'd eye,
That mocks the tear it forc'd to flow.

Gray.

SONNET XI.

LINE 4.

Float in light vision round my aching head.

Float in light vision round the poet's head.

Mason.

And the poor sea boy, in the rudest hour,

Enjoys thee more than he who wears a crown.

Wilt thou upon the high and giddy mast

Seal up the ship boy's eyes, and rock his brains

In cradle of the rude impetuous surge ? &c.

Shakespeare's Henry IV.

SONNET XII.

LINE 8.

And suits the mournful temper of my soul.

Young.

SONNET XIII.

LINE 1.

Pommi ove'l Sol, occide i fiori e l'erba.

Petrarch, Sonnetto 112, Parte primo.

SONNET

SONNET XIV.

LINE 1.

Erano i capei d'oro all aura sparsi.

Sonnetto 69. *Parte primo.*

SONNET XV.

LINE 1.

Se lamentar augelli o verdi fronde.

Sonnetto 21. *Parte secondo.*

SONNET XVI.

LINE 1.

Valle che de lamenti miei se piena.

Sonnetto 33. *Parte secondo.*

SONNET XVII.

LINE 1.

Scrivo in te l'amato nome
Di colei, per cui, mi moro.

This

This is not meant as a translation ; the original is much longer, and full of images, which could not be introduced in a Sonnet.—And some of them, though very beautiful in the Italian, would not appear to advantage in an English drefs.

SONNET XXI.

LINE 5.

' Poor Maniac.'

See the Story of the Lunatic.

' Is this the destiny of man ? Is he only happy before he pofsefses his reason, or after he has lost it ?—Full of hope you go to gather flowers in Winter, and are grieved not to find any—and do not know why they cannot be found.'

Sorrows of Werter. Volume Second.

LINE 8.

' And drink delicious poison from thine eye.'

Pope.

SONNET

SONNET XXII.

LINE I.

'I climb steep rocks, I break my way through copses, among thorns and briars which tear me to pieces, and I feel a little relief.'

Sorrows of Werter. Volume First.

SONNET XXIII.

LINE I.

' The greater Bear, favorite of all the constellations; for when I left you of an evening it used to shine opposite your window.'

Sorrows of Werter. Volume Second.

SONNET XXIV.

LINE I.

' At the corner of the churchyard which looks towards the fields, there are two lime trees—it is there I wish to rest.'

Sorrows of Werter. Volume Second.

SONNET

SONNET XXV.

LINE 1.

'May my death remove every obstacle to your happiness.—Be at peace, I intreat you be at peace.'

Sorrows of Werter. Volume Second.

LINE 11.

When worms shall feed on this devoted heart,
Where e'en thy image shall be found no more.

From a line in Rousseau's Eloisa.

SONNET XXVI.

LINE 5.

For with the infant Otway, lingering here.

Otway was born at Trotten, a village in Sufsex. Of Woolbeding, another village on the banks of the Arun, which runs through them both, his father was rector. Here it was therefore that he

probably

probably pafsed many of his early years. The
Arun is here an inconsiderable stream, winding in
a channel deeply worn, among meadow, heath
and wood.

S O N N E T   XXVII.

LINE 4.

' Content and carelefs of tomorrow's fare.'

Thompson,

S O N N E T   XXVIII.

LINE 9.

' Balmy hand to bind.'

Collins.

S O N N E T   XXX.

LINE 6.

Bindwith.

The plant Clematis, Bindwith, Virgin's Bower,
or Traveller's Joy, which towards the end of June

begins

begins to cover the hedges and sides of rocky hollows, with its beautiful foliage, and flowers of a yellowish white of an agreeable fragrance ; these are succeeded by seed pods, that bear some resemblance to feathers or hair, whence it is sometimes called Old Man's Beard.

LINE 9.

Banks! which inspir'd thy Otway's plaintive strain!
Wilds! whose lorn echoes learn'd the deeper tone
Of Collins' powerful shell!

Collins, as well as Otway, was a native of this country, and probably at some period of his life an inhabitant of this neighborhood, since in his beautiful Ode on the death of Colonel Rofs, he says :

The Muse shall still, with social aid,
    Her gentlest promise keep,
E'en humble Harting's cottag'd vale ,
Shall learn the sad repeated tale,
    And bid her shepherds weep.

And

And in the Ode to Pity :

> Wild Arun too has heard thy strains,
> And Echo, midst my native plains,
> Been sooth'd with Pity's lute.

SONNET XXXI.

LINE 2.

' Alpine flowers.'

An infinite variety of plants are found on these hills, particularly about this spot : Many sorts of Orchis and Cistus of singular beauty, with several others.

SONNET XXXIII.

LINE 9.

Thy natives.

Otway, Collins, Hayley.

SONNET

SONNET XLII.

LINE 8.

'The shrieking nightjar sail on heavy wing.'

The nightjar or nighthawk, a dark bird not so big as a rook, which is frequently seen of an evening on the Downs. It has a short heavy flight, then rests on the ground, and again, uttering a mournful cry, flits before the traveller, to whom its appearance is supposed by the peasants to portend misfortune. As I have never seen it dead, I know not to what species it belongs.

SONNET XLIV.

LINE 7.

Middleton is a village on the margin of the sea in Sussex, containing only two or three houses. There were formerly several acres of ground between its small church and the sea; which now,

by

L

by its continual encroachments, approaches within a few feet of this half ruined and humble edifice. The wall, which once surrounded the churchyard, is entirely swept away, many of the graves broken up, and the remains of bodies interred washed into the sea : Whence human bones are found among the sand and shingles on the shore.

S O N N E T   XLV.

LINE 11.

'Th' enthusiast of the lyre who wander'd here.'

Collins.—See note to Sonnet 30.

S O N N E T   XLVI.

LINE 8.

'But where now clamours the discordant hern.'

In the park at Penshurst is a heronry. The house is at present uninhabited, and the windows of the galleries and other rooms, in which there are many invaluable pictures, are never opened but when strangers visit it.

LINE

LINE 12.

Algernon Sydney.

SONNET LI.

LINE 4.

Ospray.

The sea eagle.

SONNET LIV.

LINE 12.

A sweet forgetfulnefs of human care.

Pope.

SONNET LVII.

LINE 7.

The lark—the shepherd's clock.

Shakespeare.

LINE 14.

The mountain goddefs, Liberty.

Milton.

SONNET

SONNET LVIII.

LINE 8.

'Star of the earth.'

Dr. Darwin.

LINE 9.

'The moisten'd blade—'

Wolcot's beautiful Ode to the Glow Worm.

ELEGY.

This elegy is written on the supposition that an indigent young woman had been addrefsed by the son of a wealthy yeoman, who resenting his attachment, had driven him from home, and compelled him to have recourse for subsistence to the occupation of a pilot, in which, attempting to save a vessel in distrefs, he perished.

The father dying, a tomb is supposed to be erected to his memory in the churchyard mentioned in Sonnet the 44th. And while a tempest is gathering, the unfortunate young woman

comes

comes thither; and courting the same death as had robbed her of her lover, she awaits its violence, and is at length overwhelmed by the waves.

VERSE 8. LINE 4.

'And fruitlefs calls on him who cannot hear.'

'I fruitlefs mourn to him who cannot hear,
'And weep the more because I weep in vain.'

Gray's exquisite Sonnet;

in reading which it is impofsible not to regret that he wrote only one.

THE ORIGIN OF FLATTERY.

This little poem was written almost extempore on occasion of a conversation where many pleasant things were said on the subject of flattery; and some French gentlemen who were of the party, inquired for a synonime in English to the French word fleurette. The poem was inserted in the two first editions, and having been asked for by

very

very respectable subscribers to the present, it is re-printed. The sonnets have been thought too gloomy, and the author has been advised to insert some of a more cheerful cast. This poem may by others be thought too gay, and is indeed so little in unison with the present sentiments and feelings of its author, that it had been wholly omitted but for the respectable approbation of those to whose judgment she owed implicit deference.

F I N I S.

From the Old Prefs of Isaiah Thomas, at Worcester.

Lightning Source UK Ltd.
Milton Keynes UK
UKHW051408160320
360414UK00011B/2662